T0129678

UNLEASH THE
ACTION WITHIN

Only YOU Make Today GREAT

ANDREW VASSAR

WESTBOW
P R E S S®
A DIVISION OF THOMAS NELSON
& ZONDERVAN

WestBow Press books may be ordered through booksellers or by contacting:

WestBow Press
A Division of Thomas Nelson & Zondervan
1663 Liberty Drive
Bloomington, IN 47403
www.westbowpress.com
1 (866) 928-1240

ISBN: 978-1-9736-0378-8 (sc)
ISBN: 978-1-9736-0379-5 (e)

Library of Congress Control Number: 2017915280

Print information available on the last page.

WestBow Press rev. date: 10/06/2017

Intro thought

Every morning in Africa, a gazelle wakes up,
it knows it must outrun the fastest lion or it
will be killed. Every morning in Africa, a lion
wakes up. It knows it must run faster than the
slowest gazelle, or it will starve. It doesn't matter
whether you're the lion or a gazelle—when
the sun comes up, you'd better be running.
—Christopher McDougall

I keep this quote by my desk every day. Whatever
the day has in store for me, I will be running!
www.DREWTIME.com

Contents

Introduction

In life, there are so many choices. You are in control of those choices. In every interaction, the people you let influence you will shape your life. You are a puzzle made up of a piece from everyone who has ever impacted your life. You control the pieces that remain and the path they will lead you down. Your path is the direction you are taking to achieve your goal, and with each step you take, you will need to remove and add new pieces to become the person you will need to be to achieve your goals. I want to personally thank everyone who has helped me become the person I am today. I also can't wait for the future interactions that will shape the next chapters of my life! Your mind is a masterpiece waiting to be expressed by your actions. This book is intended to be the first in a series of books to help stimulate your mind and challenge you to unlock your potential! Break free from your limitations and step into your destiny. This book is not intended to reinvent the wheel or present you with the magic cure for everything you feel is wrong. This book will not by itself make you rich. The purpose of this book is to stimulate your mind. Challenge your perceptions, and awaken the action within you. Only you can make today great!

Chapter I

YOU

You are in control of you. Your mind initiates your actions. Everything happens as a result of a choice for a specific reason. Your mind controls everything, both externally and internally. If you master your inner beast mode and control your mind, nothing outside your body can affect you. In every situation, there is a better result and a not-so-good result. It all starts with choices. You have the choice to sleep in or get up early. You choose to exercise your mind and grow your intelligence. You choose the body your mind controls. Your mind also controls the future. You can use your imagination to dream and place yourself in the future with everything you ever dreamed of. Own it, because it all starts with you.

Now step into the person you want to become. Every day, you are on stage in the movie of your life. In this movie, there are no retakes, no stuntmen, and no special effects. This isn't reality. It's life. So never look back! Become the person you will be once you hit your goals today. Take some time to envision yourself as that goal-hitting, successful person. What will you wear, how will you act, how will you talk to people, how confident will you be, and how hard will you need to work to do it bigger and greater than ever? Now act. Take on the confidence of that person. Walk and talk as that person. Dress and behave like that person. It all starts within, so make sure you are internally pumped and keep that image of your future self on repeat at all times. Use that to keep progressing toward your goals.

Your personal brand is the most important thing you have. Your brand is how people see you. It's your integrity. It's the value you hold for others. Are you always smiling? Are your clothes neat and pressed, your nails clean, your hair and face groomed and fixed? Whether you are a man or woman, first impressions and consistency are everything.

Now how do you look on the inside? Are you outgoing, smiling, laughing, and happy? Or do you need to work on that? Your brand has to be on point every day. Do not sacrifice your brand for anything or anyone. You are all you have in this world. Never devalue yourself. If you are feeling down or off, take a moment in private to reset yourself. If it is needed, go to the bathroom, look in the mirror, say something kind to yourself, wash your hands, put some water on your face, and make sure to count one, two, three. Go and get back in a prime state.

Now as to your integrity, your trust factor, integrity always starts at 100 percent with anyone you interact with. From there, based on your actions, it can remain at 100 percent or go down. Once it goes down, it can never return to 100 percent. You may achieve 99.99 percent but never 100 percent. Once you try to take a shortcut, lie, cheat, cut a corner, or fib, that person will always remember that experience. Listen to that little voice in your head saying, *Do what's right*. Then keep listening to it. It will be magical. The mind in do-good motion will be scary at first, but it will be more fulfilling and magical than anything you have experienced.

As you read or listen to this book, start to make changes, millimeter adjustments, and shifts in your life. You will start to take control and conquer. It is never too late to reinvent yourself and your brand. It must start with you. You must change your mind, behaviors, and habits first. If you do not focus internally on change, you will revert to the old you and your old brand. You can change your job, clothes, friends, car, hair, significant other, etc., but that will not help you unless you first change your mind, behaviors, and habits. How many times have you seen a person go through a negative event in life, get a new external look (gym, clothes, hair, etc.), and then go through the same negative experience a short time later? This could be personal relationships, work, school, friends, etc. You must change internally your mind first. Once you change your mind and create healthy habits and behaviors based on the motivation and goals set by your mind, then you will start to change externally.

The small changes or millimeter adjustments can be made immediately. Write down your goals, and start the change. Make sure to stay consistent with the changes and maintain them so they become routine behaviors and healthy habits. No one likes that person who makes massive changes every month or every year and overpublicizes them to everyone within earshot (or social media range) and reverts as soon as they change. When making millimeter adjustments, you do not have to tell anyone; just keep doing them consistently day after day. Those around you will notice based on the consistency and positive change. Even better, run your own race. Stop all activity on social media. Don't even look at anything on reality TV or on social media so you are not tempted to compare yourself to others. This is your life, your race, and your time. It doesn't matter where you start; it only matters where you finish. Everyone is at different stages of the life race. Stay on your path to your goals and your dreams. So many people get derailed and distracted and act like mosquitos flying around you, annoying and trying to bite you.

Life changes. Reinventing yourself is a must as you progress down your path. As we go through life, there are times when we need to change or as your parents may have told you, grow up. This is based on the choices and goals we have made. This most commonly happens between grades in school, jobs, relationships, moving, or hobbies. Remember, it starts in your mind. Do not expect others to change because of your changes. You can only control and change you. You can influence others, but they control their minds and are the only ones who can change. Don't let anyone influence your change. You can do anything you put your mind to, and you can force your body to put in an equal and greater amount of work and dedication.

Remember: (Dreams + Progress + Goals + Effort) - Laziness = Success

Kill lazy. Lazy is that voice that tells you, "No. Stop. Go back. Rest. Hit the snooze button." You know who lazy is. Recognize it. Don't let it creep into your mind and stamp out your motivation.

Motivation is what gets you started.
Habit is what keeps you going.
—Jim Rohn

Chapter 2

GO! WAKE UP!
(BEHAVIOR MODIFICATION)

The world runs 24–7 and never sleeps. For you, everything starts when you wake up. Do you get up early and jump out of bed? Are you excited to begin your day? Or do you dread waking up and hit snooze until you don't have time to take a shower or get ready properly? Are you now rushed so your clothes are mismatched and your hair is a mess? Are you angry and driving in a rush? Now you are getting angry with drivers who won't hurry for you and you drive way over the speed limit. You get where you need to go with high anxiety. You did not eat breakfast, or you made a bad choice of food. Now you are rushed to get to class or to that meeting that starts in thirty seconds. You are not prepared and look disheveled and have a poor attitude from the anxiety, stress, hunger, caffeine, and panic. People know you as that person who is always late or almost late. Remember—perception is how things appear to other people. Now your day is terrible, and it seems like everything is going wrong. You think, *This is going to be an awful day!* We all have experienced this, and we all know someone like this.

Now let's replay that same morning a different way. Maybe you are not a morning person—at first. But you will be. You plan the night before and set out clothes for the next day. You organize whatever you need for the next day. You may even think through your day, planning for the meetings and interactions you can anticipate. Maybe you will make breakfast and lunch for the next day. You wake up with time to spare. You now have a plan when you wake up. You look and feel better, your anxiety levels are lower, and you are not in a state of panic and stress all the way to school or work. You get where you are going early and are prepared and ready to attack the day.

Great. Now let's take it to the next level. Remember, progress and challenge yourself every day! Start to wake up fifteen minutes earlier every month. Use the fifteen minutes for your morning motivational routine. Get pumped up, listen to some music, read scripture, or—my favorite—look in the mirror and recite an affirmation! Picture yourself in the message. Here is one of mine:

I am the greatest. Today is my day. This is my time. I will not be denied. I am the best. I deal with owners and CEOs. I will be successful. People need what I sell. I am the best solution. This is my time. I will not be denied.

Take some time, go to www.drewtime.com, and look at affirmations and messages. Find a few that you like, and write some of your own. You may need a few based on what you are doing each day. The affirmation will also need to progress with you on your journey through life and success. Say it until you are jacked up and believe it. Train your mind, and demand that your body obey your commands. This is your morning fire-up. This is the moment before the big game of life where you need to get pumped up. Here are some examples:

- This is my day. It's going to be awesome. I will be awesome.
- Today I break through and try new adventures. Today is my day. Starting new starts today, now, with me!
- Now is my time. I am a winner. I am beautiful. I am great. Today is my day.

- It's go time. I will knock this test out of the park. I am prepared. I am ready. Today I will succeed.
- Something cool always happens to me. I am lucky. Today will be great. Today is my day.

The next month add fifteen minutes of personal time. You can use this time for whatever you would like to help increase your quality of life or progress toward a goal.

Continue to add fifteen minutes until you are waking up two hours before you must leave the house. This is a proven method to increase your quality of life, make additional income, increase your grades, and improve your life. Everyone has the same twenty-four hours in a day. No matter who you are, you only have twenty-four hours. Don't waste time. You can't get it back, and you can't save it. The difference between successful people and unsuccessful people is how much time they spend being productive and progressing toward their goals every day. Challenge yourself every day to outdo the day before. You can always reward yourself with a fifteen- to twenty-minute power nap once you hit a goal or milestone.

Here is an example of two-hour morning session to help get you started.

- Wake up at 4:00 a.m.
- Thirty-minute workout or run

- Thirty minutes to shower and get ready
- Fifteen minutes to eat and fuel the beast
- Five-minute affirmation time
- Ten-minute review calendar for the day
- Ten to twenty minutes to get my son ready
- Leave at 6:00 a.m.
- Commute time varies based on traffic. Listen to audio books and motivational speakers on YouTube. My top picks are on my website for you.
- Arrive at office 7:00 to 7:30 a.m. I avoid traffic and stress by arriving early. If something unexpected happens, such as an accident or bad weather, I have plenty of time to still make it to my office. Don't let anything derail your awesome day!

Chapter 3

CHOICES

How many choices have you made in your life? How many choices do you make in a year, month, week, and day? Now most importantly, do you track how many better or beneficial choices you pick each day versus the not-so-good choices?

In life we make millions of choices. Most of our choices do not have an immediate positive or negative impact on us. Some choices do not impact you until far in the future. Most choices build on each other. Have you ever made the choice to hit snooze? Then you must choose between skipping food, showering, or being late. When you get to where you are going, now you are starving and have missed lunch. As a result, you either spend a ton of money at vending machines or eat a super-unhealthy meal. The next result of that choice is feeling like a stuffed piñata zombie for an afternoon. Maybe you don't eat and just pound energy drinks and get a dehydration headache and are angry! They don't call it Monster for nothing. Give me a few and no water or food, and you will absolutely see a monster.

That is a simple example of how choices can have a negative domino effect on a day. That day could snowball into more depending on the influence you have had on others. Choosing to work out and eat healthy won't give you instant gratification. However, after you make those choices thousands of times, you will absolutely see a difference.

Grade yourself every day before bed. Track how many good choices you make and how many bad or not-so-good choices you make. Being aware is the first step in a change. Remember, a small good choice like a sugar-free, zero-calorie drink does not counter a not-so-good choice, like a twenty-five hundred–calorie meal. The same is true about choices and relationships. Be consistent in your choices, and keep making them. If you need to think about something, do it. It is okay to pause, take a sip of water, and reflect on your options.

The choices you make today and will make for the rest of your life shape who you are, where you are, and who you will become. If you are in a situation today that you do not like, look back on the choices that got you where you are. Now find the choices that would have corrected and changed the outcome. Great—now find a way to change your course. Make a plan, and take action. The time is now to make the changes and right choices to reach your goals. Some habits may take a long time to change, but you have your entire life to make them.

You and only you make the choices! You run your life! Don't let your actions make choices before your mind!

Chapter 4

ANTIZOMBIE—ENGAGE

One smile and the simple words, "Hi. How are you? Have an awesome day" can change people's state instantly. A simple wave in traffic can calm a frustrating and stressful situation.

We live in a world filled with technology. We have wireless everything and can immerse ourselves in the fantasy land of social media, overcommunication, and games without H2H (human-to-*human*) interaction. Do not use your phone or other technology as a security blanket or security guard.

I challenge you to keep track of all the times in a day you have the opportunity to engage and interact with someone. If you take one thing and act on it in this book, make it this one.

This looks like making eye contact and saying, "Hi, how are you? Have an awesome day." Then disengage and keep moving. Hold the door or elevator for someone. You do not have to spend more than a few seconds with someone. You do not have time. Stay on track. You need to be productive and progress past your goals.

Why engage and be nice throughout your day? One, it lowers your stress. Two, it can make someone's day. Three, you never know who someone is or how small the world is!

Here's a real story of what bad looks like. A sales rep was mad, late for a meeting, and driving like Ricky Bobby on fire. He cut off a slower driver and gave the big "you're number one" sign out the window while honking the horn, music blasting. He parked in a reserved area and got to the appointment, and guess who he was meeting? Yep, you got it. The person this sales rep gave the number-one sign to. The conversation was very brief. *Sooooo*, yeah, this isn't going to work. Bye. The sales rep had to drive an hour back to the office and explain how the meeting went to his boss and how he wasted two hours of the day and blew an important meeting with a million-dollar prospect.

Here's a real story of what good looks like. I was sitting in my car having a coaching conversation with one of my new sales reps. We were both fifteen minutes early for our meeting. We discussed the agenda, presentation, and tactics we were going to use. I explained that we were about to walk through a busy office park so we had to make sure to be nice, smile, and engage. You never know who you will meet. We engaged several people. "Hi. Have a great day." We held the main door to the high rise we were going to and the elevator for a few people. We even said, "Hi and hope everyone has a fantastic day," in the elevator! Crazy, huh? We got to the office, hit the buzzer, and were let in to sit in the lobby. As we were sitting there, a person from earlier came in. "Hi, nice to see you again." We engaged on small talk about our company and what our solutions were. Our contact came out, and we said good-bye to the other person and went to our conference room. We ran our meeting. As we were finishing up, the person came back, spoke to the person we were meeting with, and left quickly. I asked our contact who that person was. She responded, "That is the founder and president. He never speaks to anyone and never takes sales calls. He seems to like you guys and wants to be included on the next meeting." We had tried to call him hundreds of times.

Please take a moment to reflect on these two stories. No matter where you are going, there are sure to be people there. Everyone knows, works, or does business with someone. Now with social media and smartphones, the world is even closer. Smile, engage, interact, and be nice. A good friend once told me the sweet tea and heels method. She was Southern. IE look nice, act nice, and stay humble. It opens more doors and starts conversations a lot faster than being pushy and aggressive. Thank you, JC. I can't pull off the heels, but you get the point.

Be contagious in a good way. People are more attracted to a positive person. The more negative and annoying the person, the more positive you need to be. Eventually he or she will crack and you will force him or her to rise up and be positive. Be the positive tide and raise all boats to a better place. Don't be a negative wave or anchor sinking the boats. Everyone has a camera phone. Be a good story, not an embarrassment! You never know what a person has been through to get to the point where you have encountered him or her. When your path intersects another person, don't judge. You have no idea what he or she has had to overcome to get to there. Simply engage positively, smile, and lift him or her up. Your positive influence could change his or her entire day. You may energize him or her just enough to get through whatever is next on his or her journey.

It's your life. Take control. Don't
coast through on autopilot.
—Andrew Vassar

Chapter 5

MIND CONTROL (STATE CHANGE)

Every day you must conquer the demons in your mind. You must battle fear and doubt. You must fuel and motivate your body to continue to progress forward and be productive. A body at rest will desire to stay at rest and rust. A body in motion will stay in motion and attract others who will demand success. Keep moving! Keep challenging! Never lose the battle between the ears.

In an average day, you will need to change your state at least a dozen or more times. What is a state change, you ask? A state change is an emotional shift and an energy refill. An example is when I get home and pull in my driveway, I am typically on the phone in work mode. This can be high-paced and stressful or a situation that was urgent. If I don't pause and change my state before I walk into the housed I won't be in "*dad*/husband mode." I will just walk in with my mind distracted, stressed, and not at all engaged with my family. This will then project negativity. In the same way, if I have just won a massive deal and have been traveling, I cannot enter the house, yelling and popping bottles. I must take a few seconds and some deep breaths. I plan for my family and what they may be up to based on the time of day and their schedules. If it is late, they may all be asleep, and I will need to be quiet. If it is around 6:00 p.m., I know my son is going to come running and yelling, "Daddy!" I need to meet him with the same energy and swoop him up into the air. I will also need to do the same with my wife. Use a short affirmation if you need to. "Tonight will be great. It is great to be home. Family time, here we come. Let's do this."

Do not carry one state into another. Take a moment between a commute, meeting, class, hobby, interaction, etc. You are either early or late, never on time. Be early to change state. Reenergize and anticipate what will come next. Meet people where they are at and at their energy level. Come in slightly higher and more excited. Then either stay there if the other person is just as excited or lower to around their level—never below. If you encounter a negative situation or person or receive bad news, take a moment before the next thing you do, reenergize, get pumped back up, and move forward. The past is gone, and the future is not here. Live in the moments, and create the future you want. No one can stop you if you are in the right state. Most people change states like riding a roller coaster throughout the day. They are not in control. They let the environments and people they associate with change their states for them. They let one bad interaction poison their minds and ruin their entire day or even week. Do not let anything ruin your day. Every day is your day. Set your state, and keep it where you need it. You are the only one in control of your mind. You have the keys to your mind. Your mind drives your body. You do not trouble yourself with negativity, doubt, or poisoned minds.

Winning and success are mind-sets and action.
—Andrew Vassar

Chapter 6

LEADERS GO FIRST

Tell the story first. Own the story!

In every situation, there needs to be a leader. Leaders go first. But what? Why? How? You do not need a title or position of authority to be a leader. Never wait until you gain some sort of title or social status to be a leader. Create the opportunity by capitalizing on what I call the *opportunity second*. You will probably recognize it as that awkward pause. Every time there is a question asked or a volunteer to go first, there is that second of opportunity or pause. Originally your mind says, "Oh no, don't pick me." Fight the fear. It is a false interpretation of an outcome that has not happened. *Go first*, if and only if the following things are true. 1. Everyone must go. It is a lot easier to go first. That way no one steals what you are going to say. He who tells the story first owns the story. 2. If you know the right answer. 3. If you can add value to the conversation. Don't be that person who just talks to talk.

After you go first a bunch of times and accomplish one of the three things, your peers will expect you to go first. You will hear things like, "John or Jane has this for the group." You are now seen as a leader.

But wait—what if I do not know one of the three? What if I do not have the right answer, what if I can't add value, or worse, what if I don't have a good question to ask? Oh no. Leaders prepare, practice, and anticipate conversations, engagements, and opportunities. Before a meeting, class, or event, study. Learn about the place, person, or event history. Social media makes some of this easy. Also stay current on sports, news, and events in your area. Anticipate and role-play the conversation. Write down a few thoughts and questions ahead of time. If you go first, no one can take what you were going to say.

Cast the shadow of a leader. Practice your acumen. Choose your words purposefully. Speak with a purpose. Be brief, be bright, and stop (close mouth). Stand and sit with proper posture, and look the part. No one likes a sloppy, slouchy leader. In life and in racing, the air is always cleaner in the front. Look for, prepare, and capitalize on the opportunity second.

> Once you say you're going to settle for
> second, that's what happens to you in life.
> —John F. Kennedy

Chapter 7

WINNERS WIN

Winners win. A great leader once told me that winners win and keep winning. Even better, find a way to win with those around you. With everything in life, there can only be one winner in every situation—the one person who does the best, finishes first, gets the answers right, sells the most, or scores the most points. On the flip side, there is only one true looser. It is the exact opposite—the one person who finishes absolutely last and blew it. For someone to win, someone must lose. That is just how life is. However, in life you are not playing a one-on-one game like checkers. There are millions of people playing the game with you.

You may not always finish first, but you must never finish last. In everything you do, continue to set goals and overachieve them. You may not finish first in everything you do based on the circumstances. Just keep progressing toward your goal. If your scores continue to rise, your sales increase, your answers are closer to perfect, and you are moving in the right direction, eventually you will win and be first.

The upper middle is a great place. As already stated, there is one first and one last. However, there is an upper middle, call it the A-minus to B-Plus zone. This is a very comfortable zone. You are not first, but society considers you a success. Most people live their entire lives in this zone. This is the middle-class America zone. You are successful and have a great job and good social standings in your community. On paper, you are on the winning end of life. I bet you never realized it but you are not happy. You never arrive and stay happy. You must continue to progress to stay happy. That is why you pay rent on success; you do not buy it. Everyone lives up to their means or income/status and wants more. When you finally get your dream object, a few months or years later, you want something better. Funny how that always happens when you look back at your life. You may have always wanted that purse, outfit, car, house, etc. Now that you have it, a few things happen. First, you didn't reward yourself when you had the money to pay for it, and buyer's remorse sets in fast. When you act too fast and don't have the money to back it up, thanks to credit cards and loans, you start to resent the purchase or the situation. Second, after a while, you realize that whatever it was isn't all that cool and a better something is out there and more expensive.

These two scenarios are normal. They happen to everyone. The key is to recognize them and continue to move forward.

There are people who always win. Look back at your life, and I am sure you remember the people who always seemed to win. People would call them lucky, born on third base or with a silver spoon, etc. I know that you know at least one person like this. Do you think these people had more time or were born ahead of you by a genetic mutation? I do not believe so. Once a person starts winning and winning often, his or her mind-set changes. He or she expects to win. In the same group of people, such as a class or work environment, I believe that others start to believe they can't finish first or win. Whether you think you can win or you think you can't, you are right. When your mind changes and you believe you are going to win, you will do better, and more than likely, you will win. Most people are satisfied with complacency and just getting by. This helps winners continue to win.

Winners surround themselves with winners. If you are going to win, never surround yourself with losers. If you have won, move up and progress. If you are the best in a group of people doing an activity or task, go find people who are way more advanced. You will not win right away, but they will push you to continue to do better. If you work out with people who lift less weight than you, you will be stronger than them, but you will not push yourself to your limits. If you work out with people much stronger than you, they will push you, you will push you, and you will believe it can be done. If you believe you can do it, you have already beaten 75 percent of the competition. Most attitudes are, "Well, this isn't going to work, but I will go through the motions." No, believe you are going to dominate and succeed at everything you do!

Increase your wins. When you first start out with your winners win mind-set transformation, win small to win *big*. What does that mean? A race is won by every step that is taken, every lap that is completed, and every breath that is taken. You can't win a game during practice, but you will never win a game without practice. Break down everything in your life and consciously celebrate all the small wins. I bet each of you wins all day long. Here are a few examples of everyday wins. I woke up! Yeah! I am alive, winning! That is a super-easy one that you can celebrate every day. You have food, heat, a/c, clothes, and running water, all wins, or you know someone who gives you access to these things! If you are driving somewhere, celebrate not crashing. If you park between the lines on the first try (a lost art), celebrate! You can celebrate tasks. Even though being able to trip on flat ground with no apparent obstacles is a great skill, celebrate when you don't get attacked by an invisible tripping ninja and are able to walk somewhere. When you eat and don't end up wearing it on your clothes, that's a win! Break down the goals or tasks, and win each step of the way. Win by showing up on time. Win by having the right tools to participate. Win by making it through the first step and so on until you are winning numerous times before you even finish. Oh, and by the way, if you do mess up and lose at a small task, you will not feel as bad because you and your mind have already won at so much that day that it will seem trivial and insignificant. If I win one hundred times and only lose one time, I am a 99 percent winner. If I focus on the one hundred inconvenient losses or setbacks it took to get to that win and one win, I am a 99 percent failure. Winning the little things will lead to winning the big things. Winners win. Have the mind-set that you are a winner, and celebrate the wins. Track how many things you do successfully and win every day. A winning mind needs to be trained, and practice lasts a lifetime.

Chapter 8

WILL V. SKILL

The only place success comes before
work is in the dictionary.
—Vince Lombardi

Okay, this is not a new concept, and I am not reinventing
the wheel here, but stay with me. This is critical to
success. No, we cannot all be pro athletes with no
skill and all will. No, you cannot flap just your arms
and fly through will or whatever else you have read
or seen on TV. Duh, that should be obvious to every
human being on this planet regardless of what your
parents told you when you were young. We are not all
created equal. We are not all princesses, princes, and
reality TV perfect. However, everyone is given the
same chance. Everyone reading this book was born
on earth. Each of you started life the exact same way:
naked, crying, and hungry. From that moment on, it

was up to you. Yes, we each had different influencers throughout our childhood. Everyone's childhood is unique to their environment of influence. At some point, at age sixteen, eighteen, twenty-one, or even forty, we each start our own solo path without the direct influence of our childhood family or caretakers. This is when you are tested in your life works and purpose. There is yet another time in life when you will begin to influence others and decide the true path you are most fulfilled by. How far you go and how long it takes you will all be determined by your will v. skill.

Will is the gas in your tank, the blood, oxygen, energy, and mind power. Skill is your ability to maneuver your physical body in a way to produce the desired result. Without a combination of both, you will never be successful. The fastest car on earth goes nowhere without a power source. Yes, there is more than one way to power a vehicle, but it still needs power. Your will powers the skills, and the balance between the two accomplishes the goals and wins. Depending on the situation, you may need to run on more will than skill. You may be physically exhausted and run completely on will. For other tasks, you may be able to use additional skill to outmaneuver or make exciting a trivial task. It's always more fun when you drop something and are able to use your foot to flip it up to your hand and catch it. Insert the object of your choice. You know you do it or try to.

Will is the intangible powerhouse that can

completely change the outcome of a situation. Average people do not lift cars and pull people out of danger with skill. There is an imaginary switch that is flipped in their minds that triggers a full tank of *will NOS* to be injected into the will system and completely overload the physical skill. If you had the cure for cancer, you would do whatever it takes to get it to people. Nothing would stop you. Your will would overcome all objections and obstacles. When you learn to envision certain situations in your imagination, you can trigger a few extra shots of *will NOS* to propel you through the task at hand. If you are studying, imagine you are learning how cancer is to be cured and you are the only one who can retain the information needed to develop the cure. If you are working out or running, imagine a scary animal of your nightmares is chasing you or there is a heavy object trapping you. Imagine you are leading the Boston Marathon or winning a gold medal at the Olympics. How many pull-ups could you do if you were hanging off the side of a hundred-story building? I bet you could at least do one. How many of whatever (calls, tasks, meetings, etc.) could you do if your life or someone you care about life depended on it? Well, guess what it does? If your dreams were about to be realized, what would get in your way? The quality of your life and those you impact depend on you performing at your best every day. Will is 100 percent up to you. Whether you give 0 percent will or 1,000 percent will to something is completely up to you. How many times will you get up when you are knocked down? That's will.

Skill is the tangible side of the equation. Each person is born with a certain baseline for each skill that he or she needs. You might have great math skills and terrible science skills. You may be able to run like the wind but can't catch a ball very well. You may be an incredible scholar and a not-so-good physical athlete. These are just a few examples of the baselines you are born with. It would be a boring world if we were all the same. Now it is your decision as to which skills you want to develop and which you are okay with. Your heart and passion will help guide you through this process. If you are trying to overdevelop a skill that is not progressing to the level you need to measure success, your body will tell you, and you may have to make some adjustments. My suggestion is to find and focus on developing what you are good at and have passion for. If you spend all your time trying to be someone you are not or something you are terrible at, you will be miserable. Develop and focus on being the best at what you were meant to do! Your skills can be maxed out like equipment or video game characters. When they max out, they max out. Find a way to combine your skills to overcome challenges and make it happen. For example, I am not a skilled speller. If you know me, you know this. However, I want to write and influence others. Great—I use my skills for speaking and the gift of gab to talk into predictive text.

Computers are great spellers, and then it just takes a little editing. There are also numerous apps you can use to pay people to proofread. Don't let a lack of skill stop you. Find other skills you can combine to hurdle the obstacle and progress to the goal. You may invent new skills you never knew you had.

Be aware of how much skill and how much will you are currently exerting in your everyday activities. Be aware of the things you are good at. Make a list if needed. Also make a list of the things you are not so good at but need and a list of things you do not like and are terrible at. Now, spend 70 percent of your will on the good, 20 percent on the so-so, and 10 percent on the terrible. You only have so much gas in the tank every day. Use it wisely, and recognize the results and progress. You want to invest in the biggest returns. We all know someone who has all the skill in the world at something and gives 0% will and has a terrible attitude or acts like he or she doesn't care or hates it! Just imagine that they could be extremely super-talented at if they took the time to find it from a skill percent and then added 70 percent will to the mix. Boom! They would be a rock star, pro, freak of nature, or superhero!

It is that simple: recognize, focus, and empower your skills. Then supercharge them with willpower!

If you think you are beaten, you are. If you think you
dare not, you don't! If you want to win, but think
you can't, It's almost a cinch you won't. If you think

you'll lose, you're lost; For out in the world, we find success begins with a fellow's will; it's all in the state of the mind. Life's battles don't always go to the stronger and faster man, but sooner or later, the man who wins is the man who thinks he can.

—Walter D. Wintle

Chapter 9

BIG PICTURE

80 years/960 months/29,200 days/700,800
hours/42,048,000 minutes

We all hear people tell us the time is now. Don't waste
a minute. You only live once. YOLO. There are no
second chances in life. Life is too short to be unhappy.
I am sure you have heard these and thousands more
sayings. Yet many of us go to jobs we have *zero* passion
for. We have little to no money left after paying bills
and payments on things we really didn't want but
society influenced us to buy. You should get married,
have kids, get a pet, and so on and so on and so on.
You wake up miserable and are unhappy following
what everyone told you was supposed to be "living the
dream" or the "good life." We are all created uniquely
different. Your dream, what makes you happy, is not
what the norm was, is, or will ever be.

I am not saying any of the above examples are bad. I enjoy every minute with my family. However, I need you to wake up, take charge, and break the norm. Do what you enjoy, not what is expected or considered the accepted norm. I like pizza rolls and Doritos on my grilled cheese. Weird, huh? I bet a bunch of you try it and a bunch of you like it and it ends up on YouTube and Facebook. I hope I start an epic social media challenge call the "greatest weirdest grilled cheese challenge." I say that as an example of trying something new and different. I was in the kitchen one night with the entire family and *zero* money left until payday. I was angry at the world at first—oh, and really hungry. I am sure the rest of my family was too. Then I said, "I am going to make the best of this." I started looking in the fridge and the pantry. We had a ton of food. It was just a lot of canned, frozen, leftover, and forgotten foods. So we had a challenge on who could make the craziest dinner. There was only one rule. If you didn't like it, you could throw it away as long as you kept trying. It turned into a crazy night of creations like the pizza grilled cheese with Doritos; peanut butter, fluff, Nutella, banana, Lays original chips, and jelly sandwich; Hot Pocket, extra shredded cheese, instant rice, and broccoli burrito; and the fish stick, tater tot, cheese, and frozen pizza that the dog wouldn't even eat. Social media has given people a way to express the crazy or otherwise nonstandard experiments and activities in life. But how many have you tried?

Free yourself from the zombie life of blaaaaaaah. Try something different every day! Do something you truly loved as a little kid at least once per week. You are never too old, too big, or too grown up for the simple, fun things that bring pure joy. Make sure these are all PG-rated activities. Use them as rewards for making progress toward a goal. How long has it been since you had your favorite juice box, Yoo-hoo, Kool-Aid, kids' drink, etc.? Don't worry, they didn't get smaller; you are bigger. It is okay get two or three. Share one with a buddy. How long has it been since you flew a kite or played that board game you loved as a kid? What was your favorite nontechnology toy? What was your favorite outdoor activity or game? Can you still whistle, snap your fingers, cross your eyes, or wiggle your ears? Can you still jump rope, bounce a bouncy ball, play with a yoyo, or put together a puzzle? I still enjoy playing with matchbox cars and building jumps out of whatever I can find. There are several awesome things about spending some time doing what you loved as a kid. First, it is usually very inexpensive. Just don't go overboard because you can now buy everything in the toy aisles. Second, it will bring back and stimulate old memories of joy and happiness. Happy tears are all good too. Third, you will look forward to it. Make a list and write down a few things that you enjoyed as a kid. You can even make categories like food, candy, drink, toys, games, clothes, movies, shows, cartoons, etc. Get your friends and family together, and have everyone write down a few. Then get the stuff and have a fun night of activities, food, and fun from the things everyone wrote down. I am positive you will laugh so hard and have more fun than you have had in years.

Now I hope you have smiled, laughed, and elevated your mood. Life gets a little too serious these days. You are the one to determine how you live your live and how you will impact those around you. You can choose to engage and help others, smile, and be an uplifting influence. You choose to find exactly what you are looking for. If you are looking for the good in everyone, you will find it. If you believe you are lucky, you will be. The way you perceive your future will come true.

How much have you accomplished? Make a list of all the things you have done in your life. How many cities have you seen, how many people have you influenced positively, and how many times have you smiled? Now how much do you want to accomplish? Make a list of everything you want to do, see, have, influence, build, and complete. How much time do you have to complete your list? The numbers at the beginning of this chapter will be a guide for you. The average person lives for eighty years or so. How many minutes do you have left? How many minutes do you have to complete everything on your list? Never cross out anything on your list. Only add to it. Do you have a minute to spare? When someone is being negative, do you have five minutes to waste commiserating with them? When you are tired and want to sleep in for a hundred and twenty minutes, can you afford it? True wealth is how much time you have to accomplish the things you want to do. Having money buys time to do whatever you want. A great way to judge how wealthy you are is to divide all the money you have by the amount you need to live for one month. Then multiply it by thirty days. How many days can you pay yourself to do what you love? Let's do this again. Add up all your expenses and what you spend in thirty days. Divide what is in the bank by that number. You will have how many months you can pay yourself. Now multiply that by thirty days. That number is your freedom number. Your freedom number is how many days you are free to do whatever you want! When I first went through this exercise with myself, I had two hours. Remember, the key is being aware. Then your body will start to unconsciously consider your freedom cost. Your life and choices will change accordingly. Once you have a few days or a month of freedom, spend a half day or a day. Take a you day. Get inside your head, explore, try something new, go accomplish something from your list of what you want to do. Make sure to take you days. Accomplish things on your list every month. Don't wait until you are old and can't do them; start now. When you look back you want to say, "Absolutely, *yes*, I did all that." Make sure to document everything you accomplish either written in a journal, pictures, with video, or all of them. The best way to change your state when you are going through challenges is to look back at the awesomeness you have done. You will be able to use everything you have accomplished and the experiences and lessons learned to conquer anything in front of you and create the future you desire.

The front and back cover of the book of your life is already written. It is up to you to determine how many pages will be in between. What is the story going to tell? Is your story full of adventures? Is it a comedy? Would you be proud of it if your most-respected person read it? Are there a ton of blank pages filled with the things you want to do and haven't done yet? There are no lists of "I never got to this stuff" beyond the back cover. If you do not do them, they will die with you. The great thing is you are reading this book and can change the rest of the book of your life.

The game of life is simple. You are alive now, and you will die. To win the game, progress, influence, and achieve as fast as you can, putting as much distance between now and the end of the game as possible. It also helps to include food and oxygen with everything you attempt. Other than that, the world is yours. Make sure to leave the world better for the next generation to continue playing. If you see a better way show others, make it, do it, become it, and help the world progress for the better.

Twenty years from now, you will be more disappointed by the things that you didn't do than by the ones you did do. So throw off the bowlines. Sail away from the safe harbor. Catch the trade winds in your sails. Explore. Dream. Discover.

—Mark Twain

Chapter 10

TAKE ACTION

Congratulations. You have read or listened to almost the entire book. Great! What have you taken action on? What have you accomplished? What have you changed? Taking action is the most important part. You can be the most inspired, coached, motivated, excited, happy as can be, lie to yourself internally person that ever existed, and then it fades away quickly and then quicker, and you are more fake, and then the *uhhhhh*! It quite crushes everything. A book wasted. You might as well have burned the money or bought your drug of choice. Taking action and starting something immediately is the only way to begin to progress. Progress is the only way to happiness. Money and time are also great ways to initiate an action. Buying this book or audio book was an action step that initiated your investment in yourself. No matter how small the action is, always take it when you have an idea or become motivated.

Money is a great way to motivate yourself to take action. When you trade your hard-earned money for something, you will typically follow through with the action. I am sure you have booked classes, trips, gym memberships, etc. When you are having to pay for a product or service, you typically value that product or service at more than you paid. Now you have taken action. Keep doing it. Eventually it will become a daily ritual, and you will have progressed. It will then be time to take your investment to the next level.

You have a limited amount of time. If you do not schedule and organize your time, it will be wasted. If you want to accomplish something, schedule it on your phone calendar with several reminders. Make sure that your goals are scheduled and reviewed at least once per day. Take the action every time it presents itself. Immerse yourself with images, and write your goals and post them next to the bed and desk and on the dashboard of car. With only twenty-four hours in a day, your schedule is always full. Your time is valuable. How much does each hour cost you? If you invest thirty minutes on a project, book, class, or event, what was the tradeoff? Have you ever had one of those days when you wanted to get so much done, but then you didn't make a plan or schedule? You got distracted and wasted the entire day. Then just before bed, you were disappointed and felt like the day was wasted because you didn't take action! Keep your body in motion for as long as you can.

Book someone else's time. By booking someone else's time, you are almost guaranteed to take action and push each other. Having an accountability partner can be an excellent way to take action. It will also help positively influence someone else's life. Take someone or a group of people on a positive journey. When you are motivated and have a great idea, tell someone and take him or her with you. If you have someone waiting for you, you will be more likely to show up early and not miss. You will also see the other person's results and push yourself harder to achieve your goals.

Document your ideas. You only have a few brief minutes to capture your ideas and thoughts before they are lost. I am sure you have thought of something, told yourself you were going to remember it, moved onto something else, and forgotten it. Make sure to document it. Put a notepad by your bed, in your car, and anywhere else you need one. Use a note-taking app on your cellphone or tablet. Get a small voice recorder. By capturing your thoughts, you are taking action and can continue to take action in the future.

Take more action. Do not let your dreams and goals die with you. Whatever it is you want, break free and go do it. Take the action necessary to live your dreams and progress toward the life you have always dreamed of. Never worry about the opinions of the brainwashed society norms. Be you, and be awesome at it. Continue to read, learn, and educate yourself. If you continue to read one book per week for the next year on a specific topic, you will be an expert by the end of that year. Your dreams, your future, and your life are waiting for you to take action.

> The way to get started is to quit
> talking and begin doing.
> —Walt Disney

Go Now, Unleash Action, and Make It Happen Now!

Final thought: Immediate action

Read/listen to this book as often as possible. Visit my website, and take action until you have made significant behavioral change. Make a decision to commit your life to greatness. Last, pay it forward. Share as many of these books as you can, write a personal message inside, and share with as many people as possible. The more people you influence and help, the greater your life will be.

WWW.DREWTIME.COM

Action is the foundational key to all success.
—Pablo Picasso